POINTS OF VIEW

Should a College EDUCATION Be Free?

By Robert M. Hamilton

KidHaven PUBLISHING

Published in 2019 by
KidHaven Publishing, an Imprint of Greenhaven Publishing, LLC
353 3rd Avenue
Suite 255
New York, NY 10010

Designer: Deanna Paternostro
Editor: Katie Kawa

Photo credits: Cover michaeljung/Shutterstock.com; p. 5 Andrew Lichtenstein/Corbis via Getty Images; p. 7 Ricky Carioti/The Washington Post via Getty Images; p. 9 Gino Santa Maria/Shutterstock.com; p. 11 (top) sirtravelalot/Shutterstock.com; p. 11 (bottom) Antonio Guillem/Shutterstock.com; p. 13 Prostock-studio/Shutterstock.com; p. 15 Andrey Arkusha/Shutterstock.com; p. 17 Damir Khabirov/Shutterstock.com; p. 19 Syda Productions/Shutterstock.com; p. 21 (notepad) ESB Professional/Shutterstock.com; p. 21 (markers) Kucher Serhii/Shutterstock.com; p. 21 (photo frame) FARBAI/iStock/Thinkstock; p. 21 (inset, left) fizkes/Shutterstock.com; p. 21 (inset, middle-left) edella/Shutterstock.com; p. 21 (inset, middle-right) pogonici/Shutterstock.com; p. 21 (inset, right) Diego Cervo/Shutterstock.com.

Cataloging-in-Publication Data

Names: Hamilton, Robert M.
Title: Should a college education be free? / Robert M. Hamilton.
Description: New York : KidHaven Publishing, 2019. | Series: Points of view | Includes glossary and index.
Identifiers: ISBN 9781534527812 (pbk.) | ISBN 9781534527836 (library bound) | ISBN 9781534527829 (6 pack) | ISBN 9781534527843 (ebook)
Subjects: LCSH: College costs–United States–Juvenile literature. | Student loans–United States–Juvenile literature. | Education, Higher–United States–Finance–Juvenile literature.
Classification: LCC LB2342.H21812 2019 | DDC 378.3'8 –dc23

Printed in the United States of America

CPSIA compliance information: Batch #BW19KL: For further information contact Greenhaven Publishing LLC, New York, New York at 1-844-317-7404.

Please visit our website, www.greenhavenpublishing.com. For a free color catalog of all our high-quality books, call toll free 1-844-317-7404 or fax 1-844-317-7405.

CONTENTS

The Cost of COLLEGE

Learning can be expensive! Many people who go to public schools in the United States don't have to pay for their education until high school is over. However, that changes in college, which is a kind of school students can go to after high school. College in the United States generally isn't free, and in many cases, a college education can cost a lot of money.

Some people believe a college education should be free for any student who wants one. Other people strongly disagree. Read on to learn more about these different points of view!

Know the Facts!

A public college is run by a government using government **funds**. A private college is funded by individuals and isn't controlled by a government. Plans to make college free are generally only for public colleges.

Many people believe giving all Americans a free college education is the best way to help all Americans succeed. Before you decide if you agree, it's important to learn the facts on both sides of this **debate**.

A Closer LOOK

People who support the idea of free college education in the United States point to other countries that don't make students pay for college. These countries include Germany, Denmark, and Sweden.

Some U.S. states have also started **programs** that offer a free education to some students at some colleges. West Virginia and Tennessee are two examples of states that allow many students to go to a two-year public college for free. In 2017, New York began to allow some students to go to either a two-year public college or a four-year public college for free.

Know the Facts!

As of 2018, students in New York could attend a public college for free if their family earned less than $125,000 each year.

In a 2015 speech, President Barack Obama talked about the importance of free two-year colleges in the United States. He said he hoped two-year colleges would become "as free and **universal** in America as high school is today."

A Better FUTURE

Leaders who support making a college education free believe everyone should have the chance to continue their education after high school. Many people don't go to college because it's too expensive. However, a college education is needed to get many good jobs. These jobs can help people get out of poverty, which is the state of being very poor.

Income inequality, which is the difference between how much the richest people earn and how much everyone else earns, is a problem in the United States. Some people believe making a college education free for everyone can help **solve** that problem.

Know the Facts!

As of 2015, people who finished college earned 56 percent more money than people who only finished high school.

Senator Bernie Sanders, who ran for U.S. president in 2016, strongly supports making a college education free for all students. In 2017, he helped **introduce** the College for All Act. This is a plan to provide free education at public colleges for around 80 percent of U.S. students.

A Valuable EDUCATION

Many college students understand how important their education is, and they work very hard in school. However, some people believe college students only work hard because they're paying for school. They believe people take better care of things when they have to pay for them, and that includes their education.

The more money something costs, the more **valuable** it often seems. Some people argue that a college education wouldn't be seen as having as much value if it was free. They worry students wouldn't try as hard because they wouldn't be paying for their education.

Know the Facts!

A 2014 study showed that 91 percent of people who went to college believe their education was worth the price they paid for it.

Many people have argued that making students pay for college makes them take their education more **seriously** than they would if it was free.

Working Too HARD

Some people believe college students work too hard. College students often take many classes that have a lot of homework and tests to study for. Many of them join teams or clubs to make friends and be a part of their school community. They also often have jobs to earn money to pay their tuition, which is the cost of going to school.

People who support making college education free believe students shouldn't have to work many hours at a job to pay for school. This can get in the way of learning and cause them to do poorly in their classes.

Know the Facts!

A 2015 study found that more than 70 percent of college students have a job while going to school.

Working while going to college can be very **stressful** for students. This can cause them to lose sleep and not feel well.

Not Enough or TOO MUCH

Although some people think making a college education free would keep students from having to get jobs, others know that's not true. The cost of college goes beyond tuition. Students have to pay for books, food, and in some cases, a car or a place to live. Many would still need a job or a loan—money borrowed from a bank—to pay for those things.

On the other hand, there are students in the United States who can afford to pay for their college education. Many people believe these students shouldn't use the government's money for something they can afford on their own.

Know the Facts!

As of 2018, college students generally spent more than $1,200 each year on books and other supplies they needed for class.

Some people worry that making a college education free would keep young adults from learning how to **manage** their money.

Struggling with

STUDENT LOANS

Most students—or their parents or guardians—take out loans to help them pay for college. Although some people believe this teaches young adults to borrow money **responsibly**, others believe student loans are a big problem in the United States.

Student loans cause people to go into debt, which happens when people have to pay back money they owe. In 2017, the total cost of U.S. student loan debt was $1.4 trillion. Making college free would help lower that amount. Many people believe that would help the U.S. **economy**.

Know the Facts!

A 2016 study showed that 37 percent of people under 30 years old who finished college had student loan debt.

Dealing with student loan debt is a stressful part of life for many adults. A free college education could keep students out of debt in the future.

Not Really FREE

Is a free college education really free? Although students wouldn't have to pay tuition, many people argue that someone still has to pay to keep colleges running. It generally becomes the government's job to do this, and the government gets its money through taxes.

Some people worry that tuition-free college programs will cause them to pay more money in taxes to cover those tuition costs. If people are paying more money in taxes, they're not using that money to support other businesses. That's why some people believe making college free would actually hurt the U.S. economy.

Know the Facts!

As of 2016, tuition for one year at a public college in the United States cost an average of $6,613.

A free college education might sound like a great idea to many students, but it doesn't sound like a great idea to many taxpayers. Many Americans dislike having their taxes raised.

An Informed OPINION

People across the United States have taken part in the tuition-free college debate. Students, teachers, parents, government leaders, and many other Americans have shared their thoughts in favor of or against making college free for students.

Some people have strong feelings about this issue, and that can make it hard to have a respectful debate. However, it's important to understand the reasons why people on both sides feel the way they do. After learning about these reasons, do you think a college education should be free?

Know the Facts!

About 20 million students went to school at U.S. colleges in fall 2017.

Should a college education be free?

YES

- More students would go to college, which would help them get better jobs.
- Students wouldn't need to get a job to help pay their tuition and could spend more time on schoolwork.
- A free college education would reduce stress for students.
- Making college free would lower student loan debt.

NO

- Students might not work as hard in school if they were able to go for free.
- Many students would still need to get a job to pay for books and other things they need for college.
- If college was free, the government would be paying for some students who don't need help paying for college.
- Making college free requires raising taxes.

It's important to have informed, or educated, opinions about issues that will affect your life one day, such as paying for a college education. Making a chart such as this one can help you form an educated opinion.

GLOSSARY

debate: An argument or discussion about an issue, generally between two sides.

economy: The way things are made, sold, and used in a country or area.

fund: An amount of money used for a special purpose. Also, to provide money for a special purpose.

introduce: To bring something up for discussion.

manage: To look after and make decisions about something.

program: A plan of action.

responsibly: Done in the right way.

seriously: Done with care.

solve: To fix or find the answer to a problem.

stressful: Causing strong feelings of worry.

universal: Happening everywhere.

valuable: Having great worth or importance.

For More INFORMATION

WEBSITES

"Going to College"
kidshealth.org/en/teens/college.html
In this article, readers discover important things to know before they go to college.

The Mint: Fun for Kids
www.themint.org/kids/
Finding out how to pay for college is sometimes the first experience young people have with managing money, but this website helps kids understand many things about loans, banks, spending, and saving.

BOOKS

Dakers, Diane. *Money for Your Life: Invest in Your Financial Future.* New York, NY: Crabtree Publishing Company, 2017.

Hardyman, Robyn. *Understanding Credit and Debt.* New York, NY: PowerKids Press, 2018.

Steinberg, Lynnae D. *What Are Taxes?* New York, NY: Britannica Educational Publishing, 2016.

Publisher's note to educators and parents: Our editors have carefully reviewed these websites to ensure that they are suitable for students. Many websites change frequently, however, and we cannot guarantee that a site's future contents will continue to meet our high standards of quality and educational value. Be advised that students should be closely supervised whenever they access the Internet.

INDEX